The Little Flower's Mother

by the

Rev. Albert H. Dolan, O. Carm.

Founder of the
Society of the Little Flower

The Firefly Press
San Diego, California

Nihil Obstat

Lawrence C. Diether, O. Carm.
Censor Deputatus

Imprimatur

George Cardinal Mundelein
Archbishop of Chicago

FIRST PRINTING, 1927 by The Carmelite Press,
Chicago, Illinois
REISSUED, 1994 by The Firefly Press

FOREWARD

The theme of this book is aptly expressed in the words of Leonie, the Little Flower's sister,who herself became a nun. Her religious name was Sister Frances Therese. Her words, written at Father Dolan's request, are translated below:

"After having spoken with Father Dolan about my dear mother, my opinion is his, namely, that my mother was truly a saint."

On March 26th, 1994, the Holy See, recognizing the heroic virtue of Louis and Zelie Martin, declared them *"Venerable"*.

At the publication of Father Dolan's Collected Little Flower Works, in 1929, Father Lawrence Diether, Provincial of the Carmelites, wrote these words:

"Father Albert H. Dolan, O. Carm. needs no introduction, neither do his writings. The former National Director of the Little Flower Society in America, Father Dolan has become nationally known as the Champion and Promoter of devotion to little Therese . . . Fully conversant with the life of the little Saint and all its beautiful details, which the Author was able to gather on his repeated visits to Lisieux in lengthy interviews with the Saint's sisters and with all persons who had been connected with her, Father Dolan was able to give his books that personal touch of one who 'has seen and heard.'

"Father Dolan's lifework is to spread devotion to the Saint he knows so well and loves so dearly, and to win for the Teacher of 'the little way' many friends and followers among the faithful in America."

ILLUSTRATIONS

CONTENTS

Chapter   Page

INTRODUCTION

When Father Dolan made his trip to France to gather information for this little book, he was thinking about mothers everywhere whose lives would be enriched and who would draw closer to God through the influence of this remarkable mother, Zelie Martin.

As Father Dolan thought about the future, how could he see, from the early part of this 20th century, all the trials that would ravage the world? How could he have known all to which we would bear witness? The decades following this book's writing have been branded by the terrible burdens they carried: The Great Depression, World War II, Korea, Vietnam. As this book goes to press, there are wars in Bosnia and Rwanda, and untold millions of children have lost their lives before they have seen light of day, through abortion.

Throughout human history, God, in His Mercy, has raised up people who, by their lives, have personified Christianity, and through our

Catholic belief in the communion of saints, we find true and present friends among these holy people. During the Reformation, He raised up Ignatius of Loyola and Francis Xavier. From the grim prisons of the holocaust, He called Maximilian Kolbe, Titus Brandsma, Karl Leisner, Edith Stein. From the waves of immigrants who washed ashore at the turn of this century He has given us Frances Cabrini.

The most enormously popular saint of this century is still Therese of Lisieux. A re-examination of her life in the latter part of this century reveals what the plaster roses had covered up: an extraordinarily practical and brave person whose love and trust in Jesus far outweighed her immense personal suffering.

She was shaped by her home life. The love showered upon her by her mother, Zelie Martin, in the first four years of her life, was enough to carry her through her whole life. Her father, Louis, carried on this most important work after his wife's death, and devoted his whole life to simply being a good father.

These exemplary people, Louis and Zelie, have gone relatively unnoticed amidst the exultant popularity of their Therese, but, they are the tree from which this golden fruit came.

In these times, when the future is so fraught with danger, the last blessed refuge is the family. The heart of the family is the mother. Zelie Guerin Martin, whose life is chronicled in these pages, was an exemplary mother. She had an abundance of common sense coupled with a glorious delight in the spirited ways of children.

It is our hope that this book inspires mothers everywhere, and brings them a new awareness of their holy vocation, and a deepening of family hope, faith and love.

Kathleen and David Bell
San Diego, California
Feast of the Visitation , 1994

I

A Visit to the Little Flower's Mother's Home

I am going to open this book by repeating what is written in my "Living Sisters of the Little Flower," about my first visit to the home of the Little Flower's mother. I repeat the passage because it explains the genesis of this book and also because it is a fitting introduction to this biography. The passage to which I refer is: "Mrs. Grant, the custodian, took me first to the little chapel which has been built in the room in which the Little Flower was born. The room in which the little flower was born! What thoughts crowded into my mind as, after our prayers, we stood there in the little chapel room and read the inscription: 'In this room January 2nd, 1873, Therese Martin, now St. Therese of the Child Jesus was born.' How little did the Little Flower's mother guess that night of the future of her newborn girl. I thought while I was standing there of much that I had recently heard of the Little Flower's saintly mother, who had never ruled the household at Lisieux, but who died in the same room in which I was standing, the room in which the Little Flower was born. On another occasion I will tell you of the many anecdotes of the Little Flower's mother that I heard from authentic sources while I was in France and which, because they throw so much light on the Saint's mother, will not only be interesting but extremely beneficial, especially to mothers, of whom thousands in America are trying to fashion their households as much as possible after the Little Flower's family home as their model. After leaving the chapel, I stood at the head of the stairs with Mrs. Grant and said to her, 'Is this the staircase which the Little Flower used to mount, calling out at each step, 'Mama, Mama,' and refusing to mount until she heard the mother's 'Yes, Darling,' in answer?'

"'Yes, Father, it is the very same,' replied Mrs. Grant, 'I often think of that incident as I mount these stairs,' and then she added, 'The staircase has never been altered nor touched.'

"'What a patient and model mother Mrs. Martin must have been,' I said.

" 'Oh, yes Father, I often think that someone should write a book about the Little Flower's mother. What a wonderful amount of good it would do if all mothers could know intimately the mother of the Little Flower.'

" 'I had already half determined to write such a book,' I said, 'and now I have decided. If you will agree to pray that it will do the good that you have just prophesied, I will write the book and call it simply, 'The Little Flower's Mother.'

"Mrs. Grant agreed and the book will soon be forthcoming."

Now that I have explained the genesis of the present book, let me without any further preliminary begin the biography of the mother of our little Saint.

II

Her Parentage and Maidenhood

The Little Flower's mother was Zelie Guerin, a Normandy girl, born at Saint-Denis-sur-Sarthon. She belonged to one of the most Christian and Catholic families of Normandy. During the revolution her ancestors had given asylum to the persecuted clerics, and her own father, while still a boy, had not been a stranger to the ruses employed at that time by the Catholic gentry to hide the disguised priests. Her father's uncle was one of the priests who, in spite of the law which banished them, remained in the country to minister to the faithful and was often hidden at intervals in the boyhood home of her father. Later her father participated, just as did the father of the Little Flower's father, in the campaigns of the Empire and of the Restoration. He served in the infantry and then retired to Alencon after forty years of military life.

Mr. Guerin had three children, Marie-

Louise, who became Sister Marie-Dosithee in the Visitation of Mans, Zelie, who was the mother of the Little Flower, and Isidore, the youngest, who applied himself to the study of medicine.

Zelie Guerin was for a while a pupil of the Ladies of the Adoration at Alencon and at school her successes and scholarly triumphs were numerous. After her graduation she determined to serve our Lord in the person of His poor. She confided her desire to the Superior of the Hotel Dieu, but after many intimate conversation, the Superior declared definitely and without any ambiguity that such was not the will of God. One wonders how much of the basis of this decision was natural shrewdness and how much was the inspiration and revelation of God. The young lady was of course downcast and disappointed but sustained by her strong faith she waited, in the company of her parents and her younger sister and younger brother, the decision of Providence upon her life.

Her father had bought, in 1843 at No.42 Rue Saint-Blaise in Alencon, a comfortable home in which he lived with his children, but the classical studies of his son and the cost of the education of his daughters weighed heavily

upon the budget of the aged soldier. Since Zelie was destined ultimately for matrimony, she felt the need of increasing her dowry and she stormed Heaven for help. On the 8th of December, 1851, the Feast of the Immaculate Conception, she was suddenly interrupted in the middle of absorbing work, in which the play of the imagination could have had no place, by the interior voice which seemed to give her this order: "Make Alencon lace." It was the response of the Blessed Virgin to many petitions which Zelie had addressed to her.

Alencon lace is the finest in France and the only lace in the country which is made entirely by hand. Zelie Guerin studied the various steps in its manufacture and then she specialized in the assemblage of portions previously prepared, and finally she set herself to the enterprise of making the lightest and most delicate tissue. Alencon lace is made with threads of costly linen, hand-spun to an exquisite fineness.

She had under her several employees who worked in their homes, but Zelie gave the orders, furnished the designs and arranged and superintended the work. Very soon the Alencon lace of Zelie Guerin was classed among the most beautiful in the country, so that it was sold not rarely for five hundred francs a yard, the profits forming a considerable capital.

The Little Flower's Mother

III

Her Marriage and Early Married Life

Isidore Guerin, the father of Zelie, lived not far from the church of Notre Dame. A certain Captain Martin had established himself with his son Louis on Rue Pont-Neuf in Saint Peter's parish.

At this time Louis Martin, active, industrious and endowed with a very delicate artistic sense, gave every promise of becoming an expert in the jeweler's profession.

The two families (Guerin and Martin) were not acquainted. In her daily prayers Zelie Guerin again and again demanded from God to find for her a husband who would not only be a good Catholic but a fervent Catholic, and she had already with firm faith asked from God the honor of having many children who would be all in some way consecrated to God.

One day she was passing over the bridge of Saint Leonard when she saw approaching a young man whose appearance was so noble and dignified and distinguished that no one could but bestow upon him a second glance. She did not know him, but an interior voice manifested to her once again the solicitude of God over her life. The voice said: "It is this young man that I have selected for you."

Not long afterward under circumstances that have not been revealed, Zelie Guerin and Louis Martin were introduced and finally united in the bonds of matrimony in the church of Notre Dame in Alencon on the thirteenth of July, 1858. Their home was upon the Rue Pont-Neuf. The husband continued his chosen profession and Zelie her manufacture of Alencon lace and the clientele of both became numerous and their material future was assured.

The newly married couple felt increasingly each day the benefit of their mutual labors. To her practical sense and rare energy and increasing activity, Mrs. Martin joined an admirable spirit of the deepest faith. One ambition dominated her life: she had appropriated for herself this maxim of Saint Francis, "Labor, that in all things God may be better loved."

Mr. Martin's character was perhaps more

calm and quiet. He had by nature a very marked taste for religious contemplation and he was a model of patience and alert charity which gave to their common life a charm which every day increased.

The intimacy of the union between the two spouses expressed itself most remarkably in the service of God and specifically in their love of our Lord in the tabernacle, for every morning they assisted together at half past five mass. They knelt together at the holy table, and although at that time frequent communion was not practiced in France, they received Holy Communion more often than once a week. In spite of the absorbing work of the husband and the fatiguing labors of the wife, Mr. and Mrs. Martin observed rigorously the fasts and abstinences of the Church, although they lived at a time when the spirit of mortification had become enfeebled in the better French families.

This spirit of faith manifested itself even more touchingly in the intimacy of the home. Prayers were always said in common, the young couple always endeavoring to place into the "Our Father" the heavenly fervor of Captain Martin (the soldier father of the Little Flower's father; observe the military ancestry of both the father and mother of the Little Flower), whose recitation, it is said, no one could hear without tears. The Lives of the Saints were read every evening in their home and in these lives the couple must have recognized kindred spirits.

One day as the young wife was reading the biography of Madame Acarie who, after having given her children to Carmel, consecrated herself to God in religious life, Mrs. Martin exclaimed; "All her daughters Carmelites! Is it possible that a mother could have so much honor?"

Since this was the spirit of the wife it is easy to understand why she approved so strongly the practice of her husband, the practice of giving one entire night each month to prayer before the Blessed Sacrament. Often she accompanied him on walks into the country, where they were wont to end every walk in some church kneeling happily before a tabernacle too often deserted.

Mrs. Martin was always ready to relieve the miseries which came to her notice. One of her servants was taken ill with articular rheumatism. The servant's parents were poor and could not procure for her the necessary medicines and nursing care. Mrs. Martin devoted herself therefore night and day for several weeks to the care of the servant until she was entirely well.

Nothing was wanting in this family of true Christians except the power of transmitting their virtues to a numerous posterity. God answered the prayers of Mrs. Martin and magnificently blessed his two faithful servants by giving them within a few years nine children. They wished that each one of their little ones from their entrance into this world should be consecrated to the Queen of heaven, so they gave to each of their children the name of Mary. Marie Louise (Marie Louise, the eldest, is the only one of the daughters who was not called familiarly by the family by her second name. She was always called simply Marie), Marie Pauline, Marie Leonie, and Marie Helene, were the first four children to come to increase the joy of their home.

But the parents in their desire to multiply here below the Glory of God demanded of him through the intercession of St. Joseph "a little missionary." They thought that their prayers had been answered when to the little girls, who already filled the home with laughter and song, was added a little brother who received the name of Marie Joseph Louis. Alas! He had hardly time to smile at his mother; for, five months after his birth, he took his place among the angels to intercede for his terrestrial family. Prayers and novenas were redoubled with great fervor. They must have, at any price, a priest, a child who would become a great saint. Again their prayers seemed to be answered in the person of Marie Joseph John Baptist who also soon went to heaven to fulfill the mission that God had refused him here below.

After this, Mr. and Mrs. Martin believed that their prayers were not to be answered; they consoled themselves by recalling that the ways of God are not our ways and they did not ask any longer for a missionary, but who shall dare to affirm, considering the future history of one of their children that God had rejected their prayers?!

When the two older sisters, Marie Louise, who, being the eldest was always called Marie, and Marie Pauline, became old enough for school, they were sent to Mans under the care of the Visitation Sister of Mrs. Martin, Sister Marie Dosithee.

To defray the expenses of their education and at the same time to keep their home supplied with comforts, the courageous mother resolved to apply herself with new energies to the further development of her commerce in lace. She accepted large and numerous orders, gave long hours to the instruction of her employees, carried on a vast commercial correspondence and filled the house with activity.

There was no room for recreation. She writes to her brother's wife, September 28th, 1872: "To tell the truth the only pleasure I have is to sit by my window and assemble my Alencon lace." (Author's note. One entire afternoon the author sat by the very same window talking with the custodian of the home, Mrs. Grant, about the Little Flower's mother.) Nevertheless she enjoyed keenly the charms of family life; they were almost her only earthly joys and she applied herself with simplicity, good grace and devotion to the fulfillment of all the duties of motherhood.

Mrs. Martin had, as we have said, a brother, Isidore Guerin, who before becoming the grand Christian man who was later the father of Marie and Jean Guerin, had been for a moment entranced, in the course of his medical studies, by the allurements of Parisian life. It was at this time of temptation that the Little Flower's mother wrote to her brother Isidore the following letter:

"My dear brother:

I am greatly disturbed about you. My husband every day makes many sad prophesies concerning you. He knows Paris and he tells me that you will suffer temptations which you will not be able to resist because you have not enough piety. He tells me that he, himself, underwent those temptations and that he had need of great courage to emerge victorious from the battle. If you only knew or if I could only tell you the temptations through which he passed! I beg of you, my dear brother, to do as he did. Pray, and you will not be swept away by the torrent. If you succumb once you are lost. It is only the first step that counts on the way to evil just as in the way of good; after that one is swept along with the current. If you will only consent to do one thing that I am now going to ask of you, I will be more happy than if you were to send me all

Paris. This is it: you live very near the church of Our Lady of Victory. Very well. Enter there just once a day and say just one "Hail Mary" to our Blessed Mother. You will see that she will protect you in a very special way and that she will promote your success in this world and give you afterwards an eternity of happiness. That which I ask of you and promise you, my dear brother, is not due to any exaggerated piety of mine, nor is it without foundation, for I have reason to have confidence in the Blessed Virgin. *I have received from Her favors that I alone know.* You know well, my dear brother, that life is not long. You and I will soon be at the end, and then we will indeed be happy to have lived in such a way that our last hour may not be bitter."

How much that letter reveals of Mrs. Martin's character, and is that letter not indeed a sermon in itself, a sermon on the brevity of life, and upon the efficacy of prayer, especially to the Blessed Virgin in times of temptation against holy purity?

Her brother so well profited by Mrs. Martin's advice, that soon, having established himself at Lisieux as a pharmacist, and having married the pious Madamoiselle Fournet, he became one of the most practical and militant Catholics of the region.

After his marriage, a very close intimacy existed between the Martins in Alencon and the Guerins in Lisieux. It was at Lisieux, at her brother's home and accompanied by her children that Mrs. Martin spent those rare holidays that she permitted herself. It was to her brother's wife that she addressed most of the letters, as simple as they are distinguished, in which she traces so many charming tableaux of her family life and in which expressions of supernatural hope mingle with the tears of her troubles. These letters*, preserved by Mrs. Guerin and afterwards recovered by Mrs. Martin's daughters are a precious mine of information concerning the Little Flower's mother, and some of these letters which so well reveal her character are reproduced on the following pages.

Mrs. Martin never permitted her brother to forget that she was his older sister, and that

*These letters were obtained by Father Dolan through the Little Flower's sister, Pauline, and are here published in English for the first time. [Author's Note.]

she therefore had a right to moralize in her letters to him. One day a rich lady of the village remarked to Mrs. Martin: "Oh how happy I am. I lack nothing. I have health; I have wealth; I can procure for myself and do procure for myself all that I desire. I have no children to trouble my ease and my repose. In fact, I do not know anyone who is more fortunate than I."

Mrs. Martin made these remarks the text of the following letter written to her brother on March 28th, 1864: "I must say to you, my dear brother, that thrice unhappy is he who utters or cherishes such sentiments. My dear brother, I am so persuaded of the truth of what I say that at certain times in my life when I had reason to believe that I was happy I could not think of it without trembling, for it is certain, and often proved by experience, that happiness is not found here on earth and that if by chance one enjoys happiness for a while it is but a prelude to some catastrophe. I have experienced that often myself. No, my dear brother, happiness is not found here below and it is a bad sign when all prospers. God in his wisdom has thus arranged life so as to make us remember that earth is not our true home."

Her Marriage and Early Married Life

Her letters are not all filled with this high moralizing; many are very gay recitals indeed of the doings of her children, who play about the table on which the lace is being made; others contain expressions of the great spirit of thanksgiving that overflows the soul of the young mother as she views the treasures that had been confided to her. For instance, she had placed her last born, Helene, in charge of a nurse and she naively expresses her maternal joys in a letter to her brother on April 23rd, 1865: "I went to see Helene yesterday. I do not remember ever to have experienced a throb of happiness like that which came at the moment that I took her in my arms. She smiled at me so graciously that I thought I was seeing a little angel. My little Helene, when shall I have the happiness of possessing her permanently! I cannot realize that I have the honor to be the mother of so delicious a little creature."

Alas! the little one, five years later, was to flee forever the arms of its mother and leave in that heart, the love in which is so plainly revealed in the lines just quoted, an incurable wound.

A less remote sorrow came now as a

prelude to many others which awaited Mrs. Martin. Captain Martin, her husband's father, died, on which occasion she wrote on June 27th, 1865, to her brother: "My husband's father died yesterday at one o'clock in the afternoon. He had received the last sacraments the day before. He died like a saint. As was his life, so was his death. As one lives, so shall he die. I would never have believed that his death could have so affected me. I am desolate."

She was soon to become all too familiar with the spectacle of death. In the years immediately following her father-in-law's death, her two sons died as we have already indicated. Then came the death of her own father, on which occasion she wrote to her sister-in-law on the third of September, 1868: "If you only knew how holy a death he had. I hope, in fact I am certain, that my dear father has indeed been well received by the good God. I only wish that my death will be like his. I already have had masses said for him, and soon we shall have many more. His tomb will be near that of my two little Josephs."

On the following first of November she wrote to her brother: "If the good God has heard me, our dear father is today in paradise. Our poor dear father—he was not accustomed to suffer. As for me I am not at all frightened at going to purgatory; it is entirely natural for me to suffer. If the good God wishes I shall, as I have told Him, suffer my father's purgatory as well as my own. I shall be content to know that he is happy."

To these sorrows was joined the anxiety caused her by the frail constitution of Leonie, her frequent illnesses and certain difficulties that her education caused.

This mother, who in spite of her exquisite sensibility, had valiantly endured such trials and who was strengthened rather than weakened by grief, was also able to bear without complaint the thousand and one difficulties and annoyances of the busy household.

But to her cares as mother, wife and employer, there was now added her fears for the health of her sister, the Visitation nun, who now was threatened with tuberculosis.

She was the more afraid of losing her sister because Pauline and Marie had progressed marvelously under the direction of the Visitation Sister, Mrs. Martin's blood sister, and their budding virtue had been her chief consolation in the midst of many trials.

Marie was shy and reserved, and underneath her timidity was hidden a heart of gold.

Pauline was gracious and thoughtful, endowed with great talent, and was the joy of her teachers.

It was after the death of her father that Mrs. Martin began to value more highly the sweet and happy dispositions of Marie and Pauline and to realize the consolation that their amiable qualities could give to her in her trials.

She induced Marie to offer for the soul of her grandfather the pain of a certain dental operation. "This morning at eight o'clock," writes Mrs. Martin to her brother on January 5, 1869, "I took Marie to the dentist. She asked me if the operation would really help her grandfather. Upon my affirmative response, she did not cry at all in the chair and was so quiet that the dentist said he never saw so determined a child. This new examination of her tooth proved the operation to be unnecessary and the little tot then said to me, 'It is a pity; if it had been necessary, my poor grandfather would have been released from Purgatory.'"

In return for the pious education she gave her children, this Christian mother tasted even amidst severe trials the most comforting consolations of our faith. God planted some flowers in the rough path which she walked, but before she reached the end there were other trials in store for her.

On the 23rd of February, 1870, Mrs. Martin buried her fourth child, the little Marie-Helene. The others who died were Marie-Melanie and the two Josephs. After the death of Marie-Helene, the Little Flower's mother wrote on October 17th, 1870, to her sister-in-law, this letter:

"When I closed the eyes of my dear little children and prepared them for burial I was indeed grief-stricken, but thanks to God's grace I have always been resigned to His will. I do not regret the pains and the sacrifices which I underwent for them. People say to me, 'It would have been much better if you had not given birth to those whom you lost so soon after their coming.' I cannot endure such sentiments. I do not find that pains and sacrifices can at all outweigh or compare with the eternal happiness of my little ones, eternal happiness which, of course, would never have been theirs had they never been born. Moreover, I have not lost them for always. Life is short. Soon I shall find my little ones again in heaven."

Would that every mother and father could read that last letter. Surely its lessons are obvious; it needs no comment. Just let us recall that it comes from the pen of one whose last and ninth child became the great Saint Therese. If Mrs. Martin had been innoculated with certain current views, the world would never have been blessed with the fragrance of the Little Flower.

Towards the end of 1870 Mr. Martin gave up his jewelry business to one of his nephews in order to help more directly and actively his wife's lace business which had taken on enormous proportions.

An era of great prosperity opened for the family, when suddenly there came an invasion of Alencon by the victorious Prussians. Mrs. Martin had to open her home to nine Germans who, though they avoided the more odious forms of violence, destroyed in a twinkling of an eye the good order established by the mistress of the home. She writes: "They put my furniture into a terrible state. The town is in desolation. Everyone except ourselves is in tears."

At this unhappy time Mrs. Martin's husband manifested the same courage as his valiant wife, as she herself is happy to testify in this letter: "Possibly men from forty to fifty will be drafted. If my husband goes I am prepared; I expect it and he is not concerned; he says often that were he free he would like nothing better than to enlist."

At this time when a wife of the town had tried to hide her husband after he had been drafted by the order of mobilization, the heroic mistress of the Martin household wrote: "How is it possible that anyone could do such a thing?"

The war was ended before Mr. Martin was called to the colors. After the war the family moved from their home on the Rue du Pont-Neuf to a house on the Rue Saint-Blaise. This property had become the heritage of Mrs. Martin upon the death of her father and the home was destined to be the birthplace of the Little Flower. Celine had been born in the former home the year before, 1869. At this time the mother wrote: "Four of my children are already well placed (she refers to the four who had gone to heaven) and my other children will go also to that heavenly kingdom, laden with greater merit for they will have fought a much longer time."

See how Christian hope always assuaged her sorrows and gave her that remarkable tranquility and spirit of resignation so discernible in her letters.

IV

The Birth and Infancy of St. Therese

The two admirable Christians, Mr. and Mrs. Martin, now enjoyed in their new home several years of pure joys and intimate felicity. It was into this atmosphere of peace and piety and tenderness that there came January 2nd, 1873, another baby hailed as the others had been with transports of joy. This time it was the little missionary, the object of so many vows and ardent prayers: Therese, the frail little missionary who all unknown to her parents was to win to God more souls than the most renowned apostles.

This night Pauline and Marie were home on vacation and were sleeping in a room on the second floor when their father mounted the stairs with a light step announcing joyously, "My children, you have a little sister."* (See footnote on the next page.)

Then kneeling, the daughters and the

father gave fervent thanks to God.

Marie, the eldest sister, was chosen as the godmother of the Little Flower. The godfather, a son of a friend of Mr. Martin, lived at some distance and his coming was so tardy that Mrs. Martin was greatly disturbed and beseeched God not to let her little daughter die without baptism. Finally, January 4th in the afternoon, all the family went to the church of Notre Dame for the baptism. In accordance with the vow of her parents, the little one received, like her other sisters, the name of Marie to which was joined Therese, the latter name prevailing in the usage of the family.

Therese, pure as a starry sky and white as snow, carried in the arms of Louise, the domestic of the family, regained her home, while the

*Some may perhaps think that the details given concerning St. Therese are too minute and abundant. The canons of rhetoric might require abridgment but the avidity of lovers of the Little Flower for all that concerns her has made me believe it would be well to penetrate as far as possible into the intimacy of that home which was so worthy of her. [Author's Note.]

bells of Notre Dame sounded a joyful melody. Mrs. Martin was reassured now and content.

The weeks rolled by, illumined by radiant hopes. The mother resolved to nurse the child herself, for she thought that she discerned already a halo radiating divinely from the forehead of the little one. Once the mother, singing to the child, thought for a moment she heard the little one also feebly sing. Whether or not she did sing, the presage would be verified, for that soul, who just made its appearance into the Martin home, became indeed one of the world's greatest singers, singing God's mercy and goodness so sweetly that all the world has paused to listen. But soon the strength of the little one began to decline, and she seemed destined to follow to Heaven the other four Martin children who had died in infancy. A new sorrow seemed about to come to the poor parents. The family physician did not conceal from them that the only possible remedy for the little one was to confine her to the care of a vigorous nurse.

Mrs. Martin had already employed as a nurse for one of the other children a strong peasant woman, Rose Taille, herself the mother of many children. Mrs. Martin resolved to try the remedy counselled by the doctor and she writes to her brother's wife in 1873: "If it had not been so late I would have set out that night to find the nurse. How long the night was! Therese would not take the least nourishment and during the night all the sad signs that preceded the death of my other little angels manifested themselves and I was sad at heart that my poor little last-born could not receive from me the least help in her weakened condition.

"At dawn I set out for the country to see the nurse. She lived on a farm three miles out of Alencon. I went myself because my husband was away and I was unwilling to trust my mission to any messenger. On the deserted country road I encountered two rough looking men who inspired in me a little dread, but I said to myself, 'If they kill me it makes no difference; I have the death of grief already in my heart.' Arriving at the home of the nurse I asked her to come to our house immediately. She replied that she could not leave her own children, but that she would come and bring Therese back with her to her farm and care for her there. Knowing that my little one would be safe and in good hands I consented."

The two women returned together to Alencon before noon and at the sight of the dying infant the nurse shook her head discouragingly as if to say, "It is too late."

Mrs. Martin, utterly cast down by the livid color of the little Therese, went to her room, threw herself on her knees before a statue of St. Joseph and between her sobs invoked that patron of desperate causes.

Then after her prayer, she descended the stairs and lo! the child at the breast of the nurse seemed to have taken new life and courage. But it was but the happiness of an instant. Definitely overcome now by the malady, the little Therese fell back on the lap of her nurse and lay there immovable without breathing, without any sign of life whatsoever. Thinking the child was dead, the poor mother amidst her tears found in her faith and piety enough courage to thank God at that moment for the peaceful death of her innocent one. But lo! just then the little one reopened her eyes and smiled long and sweetly upon the thankful mother. This time St. Joseph had done his work. Therese in a few hours was well enough to be carried to the country in the arms of her nurse.

There are extant some letters written by Mrs. Martin at this time, describing her visit to Therese at the farm home of the nurse. March 30, 1873, she writes to her brother's wife in Lisieux: "Up until last week Therese had been quite well and had even grown quite plump, but since last Friday she is suffering from an irritation of the intestine and when the doctor came he found her in a high fever. Nevertheless, he tells me that he does not believe there is any danger. Today she is better, but I have serious fears. I cannot but think that she will not live. I have done everything possible to save my little one, and now if the good God disposes otherwise, I will try to endure as patiently as possible the sacrifice He asks of me."

Then at this time, other trials came to Mrs. Martin. While Therese was still ill, Marie returned ill from school and was stricken with typhoid fever. For long weeks she languished at Alencon under the eyes of her mother. Mrs. Martin gave to her care most of the hours of the day and often of the night. At the same time, she superintended the work of her lace workers. The poor woman bent under the burden, but her faith never wavered.

April 13, 1873, she wrote to her brother's wife, who had suffered a great material loss through fire: "Everyone has his cross to bear, but there are some who find the cross heavier than do others. You have just commenced to learn, my dear sister, than all in life is not roses. The good God sends suffering to us in order to detach us from earth and raise our minds to Heaven.... I do not ever leave my sick Marie and I sleep beside her nights. Under my present burden, I am sure that a special grace from God has been necessary and has been given to save me from collapsing under it."

At this time, Mr. Martin undertook a pilgrimage of penance to win Marie's cure. On May 3rd, Mrs. Martin wrote to Pauline: "Your father left early this morning to make a pilgrimage for Marie. He left fasting and will return fasting in an effort to persuade the good God to hear his prayers. He will make the journey on foot, returning tonight about midnight."

God indeed heard the supplications of the parents for their two sick daughters. Slowly, and after frequent relapses, Marie became convalescent. Therese recovered from the intesti-

nal malady, and on May 5th, the mother wrote
this reassuring news to Pauline: "Last Sunday,
Rose, the nurse, without notifying us, brought
Therese to our house. We were not expecting
her and at 11:30, just as we were seating ourselves at the table, Rose entered accompanied
by four of the children and with Therese in her
arms. Rose immediately gave the little one to
me and then departed for mass. But that depar-
ture did not please the little one at all. She cried
until I thought she would suffocate. The whole
household was in an uproar. It was necessary to
dispatch one of the servants immediately to the
nurse, to tell her to return here with all speed
after mass. The nurse came in soon; she had
rushed all the way from church. The baby was
immediately consoled and became quiet. We
were all surprised to find Therese so strong."

What consolation for Mrs. Martin after
the fears and anxiety of the first months, to be
finally assured that Therese would live and wax
strong.

Again, two weeks later, Mrs. Martin
wrote to Pauline: "Thursday I saw the little
Therese. Her nurse brought her but Therese did
not wish to stay with us, and sent forth piercing

cries when she could no longer see her nurse. Louise, one of the servants, had to take her to Rose who was downtown selling her butter, and as soon as she saw her nurse, Therese began to smile and there was no more crying at all. She weighs 14 pounds and she will be very gentle and later very pretty."

The acts of the infant Therese differ little from those that all mothers can observe, but in the two following letters, the mother declares that she seems to have observed the first unusual manifestations of the presence of the Holy Spirit in the little innocent soul. The first letter was written November 30th, 1873, when Therese was nine months old. Her mother, writing to Pauline, is describing the physical development of the Little Flower, and mentions the first reflection on the baby's countenance of the presence of divine grace in her soul. "I hope that little Therese will walk by herself in five or six weeks. Even now if we place her upright near a chair, she will hold herself up well and never fall. She takes little precautions against falling and seems very intelligent. I believe that her appearance will be better than the average. She smiles continually and has the expression of a predestined one. Never have I seen such an expression in your countenance or that of the older ones."

On the following January 11th, Mrs. Martin writes: "Since last Thursday my little Therese walked all alone. She is as sweet and delicate and pretty as a little angel. Her disposition is charming; I can see that already. How sweet her smile is! I long for the time when she can stay with me here at home."

Is it not remarkable to see this feeble child, hardly a year old, manifesting already by the sweetness and grace of her countenance the presence of the hidden God who has taken his delights in her soul.

Rose, the nurse, brought Therese home permanently on April 2, 1874.

Now the calamities that threatened the Martin home seemed definitely averted. Marie had entirely recovered her health; Pauline continued to be the pride of her teachers and the consolation of her mother; the little Celine, vivacious and amiable, had not seriously suffered from certain illnesses that had inspired fear for a time; Leonie was making satisfactory progress at school. The two spouses forgot their recent agony in the midst of the caresses with which childish hands showered them. The Little Queen was the source of constant delight. Mrs. Martin wrote to her brother's wife January 1, 1874: "None of my children was so strong, except perhaps the first. She will be beautiful. She is already gracious and graceful. I admire her little mouth which, as the nurse says, is 'as small as an eye.'"

In the midst of these joys, Mr. Martin did not forget the duty of thanksgiving. In 1873, after the cure of his daughter, Marie, he went to make his Thanksgiving at Notre Dame de Chartres. In October he went to Lourdes with a diocesan pilgrimage and to these pilgrimages of thanksgiving the fervent Christian joined the most assiduous perseverance in his habit of monthly nocturnal adoration of the Blessed Sacrament.

On her part, Mrs. Martin, surrounded by pious children who gave early signs of religious vocations, stimulated in the way of piety and abnegation by her holy Visitation sister, applied herself more fervently than ever to become more intimately united with God. In the following letter, written November 1, 1873 (the eve of the

Feast of All Saints), Mrs. Martin confides to Pauline and Marie, now reunited in the Visitation School at Mans, her determination to progress further in virtue: "I must now go to vespers to pray for my dear departed parents. There will come a day when you will render a like service for me, but I must so live that I will not have too great need of your prayers. I wish to become a saint. That will not be easy; there is indeed much to hew down and the wood is hard as stone. It would have been better to commence sooner when it would have been less difficult, but better late than never."

Of course, this is the language of humility, for as those who have followed her life so far and have read her letters know, she had long before this been far advanced in the struggle towards perfection.

God, who had designs on the Little Therese, seemed to use, to preserve her, means that sometimes seemed to defy the laws of nature. The following facts recounted by Mrs. Martin in her letter of June 25, 1874, presents an example of God's providence over Therese: "Recently, I had a singular adventure with my little one. I go to mass at half-past five. I did not dare at first to leave Therese alone but seeing that she never awoke, I decided to push her crib so close to my bed that it would be impossible for her to tumble out. One morning, I forgot to move the crib. When I returned, and entered the bedroom, I did not see my little Therese.* At that moment, I heard a little cry and I saw her sitting on a chair near the bed, her head resting on a pillow. I cannot understand how she could have fallen from the crib into the chair. I have thanked the good God for preserving her from any harm. It was indeed providential, for ordinarily an infant would have fallen to the floor. Her angel guardian had watched over her and the souls in purgatory to whom I had said prayers every day for her, protected her."

Therese manifested in a manner as charming as naive, a tender affection for her mother, and Mrs. Martin smiles deliciously at these manifestations of filial affection. She writes in 1874 to her two elder daughters, Marie and Pauline: "Picture the baby embracing me and passing her little hand over my face. I could see that she was greatly interested. The poor little one will

*Therese was then about one year old.

56

not leave me; she is continually with me. She loves especially to go into the garden, but if I am not there, she will not stay there and cries until I return or until she is brought to me."

The pious mother was soon to experience through Therese joys more profound. Mrs. Martin had wished that the little one's first words should be words of prayer, and on the 18th of November, 1874, the little girl, hardly twenty-two months old, offered to "the good Jesus," the love of her child's soul and this in such terms and with such an accent that the mother was delighted. She writes to Pauline and Marie who were at school: "My little Therese becomes daily more and more sweet and gentle. She gurgles and hums from morning until evening. She sings us little songs but it is necessary to be accustomed to her to understand them. She says her prayers like a little angel. It is ideal."

Soon Therese was taken to church, and it was wonderful to see the attraction that this child of two years manifested for the mass, of which one would almost say she had already feebly divined the import. Let us listen to her mother describe her at this time; no one is better

fitted than Mrs. Martin to be a witness to the
action of divine grace on the little soul. The
mother writes to her brother's wife, March 14,
1875: "Therese looks and is well. She carries on
with us the most amusing conversations. She
knows her prayers. Every Sunday she goes to
vespers and if by chance we cannot take her, she
cries inconsolably. Some weeks ago, on a Sunday, it was raining. She started to cry, saying
that she had not been 'to mass.' Unobserved for
a moment by us, she opened the door and in the
pouring rain started down the street in the
direction of the church. I ran after her and
brought her back, and her sobs continued for a
good hour. She says to me very much aloud in
church, 'Mama, I have prayed well to the good
God.' When she doesn't see her father say his
prayers in the evening, she asks, 'Why, Papa, do
you not say your prayers? Have you been to
church?' Since Lent began, I go to the six o'clock
mass, and she is often awake when I leave, and
says to me, 'Mama, I will be very good.' And she
doesn't move until I return."

This little two year old girl, so inclined
towards the things of God as to wish to go to
church in the pouring rain, revealed to some

extent by this unusual courage, the attraction for God which led the Holy Spirit to invite her to "refuse nothing to Jesus."

Mrs. Martin enjoyed to the full these first supernatural flashes upon the life of St. Therese that we have so far related, but these joys of the Christian were not unmixed with the anxieties, though passing, of the mother. Therese struck her forehead against a table and the accident caused a wound which the mother at first feared would mark the little one for life. Then again Therese scarcely recovered from one severe cold when she contracted another. But after these little troubles, the clouds lifted and smiles came once more to the mother.

The Little Flower's Mother

V

The Mother During the Girlhood
of St. Therese

For some time now, the family enjoyed tranquil happiness. There exists a picture of the family, the children gathered about their parents in the sitting room of their home. The picture was taken one evening, probably in September, when Marie and Pauline were home on vacation. Under the brilliance of a lamp, each one is occupying or recreating himself according to his peculiar inclination. The father, whose grave countenance is already surmounted by white hair, has brought his paper, but he is more occupied with his children than with the news of the day, and is conversing with Leonie who is doing some scholastic work in preparation for the opening of school. Marie is leaning on the back of a large chair in which Mrs. Martin is seated. The mother is watching the little Therese who, kneeling against the mother's knee with hands joined and her eyes raised to Heaven, is addressing "the little Jesus," Whom one would imagine she saw. Celine, also on her knees, mingles her prayers with those of her little sister who was always her playmate and companion. Pauline, always occupied seriously, interrupts her reading to smile at the angelic infant in conversation with God. What a delicious scene! How well it reveals the tastes and patriarchal customs of that most Christian family. Is it any wonder that God blessed that home with a saint?

The Martin family circle was not entirely closed to outsiders, but they mingled habitually with scarcely any but close relatives. Mrs. Martin's intimacy with her brother, the reader already knows. The better Mrs. Martin came to know her brother's wife, a woman of piety and character, the closer friendship between them became, and Mrs. Guerin became the confidant of the joys and sorrows of Mrs. Martin. The Martins went frequently to visit the Guerins in Lisieux, not because Mrs. Martin was really anxious for relaxation, but because she knew how Celine and Therese loved to play with their sweet little cousins, Marie and Jeanne Guerin.

Once Mrs. Martin went to visit her sister, the Visitation Nun at Mans. The days of the Sister, afflicted with tuberculosis, were numbered, and Mrs. Martin wished to present to her sister Therese who, having given such early signs of piety, might one day, who could tell, occupy a place in the choir of cloistered religious. Mrs. Martin writes to Mrs. Guerin of this visit in the following letter dated April 29, 1875: "My little Therese was very happy to take the train. Arriving at Mans she sat in the parlor of the convent as serious as a big girl. Then, I do not know what was the matter, she began to cry noiselessly, the big tears rolling down her cheeks. Maybe it was the grille that caused her fright. Soon she stopped crying and when my sister came she replied well to all questions as if she were taking an examination. The Mother Superior came to the grille, and I said to Therese, 'Ask the good Mother to give you her blessing.' Therese replied, 'My mother, do you want to come to my house.' And at this, of course, everybody laughed."

Therese, as the reader doubtless knows, was not entirely exempt from little outbursts that revealed her willful temperament, but Mrs.

Martin watched over her carefully, insisted upon perfect obedience, and warned her husband when, during the first few months, she thought he showed a tendency to humor and spoil Therese, "his little queen." One evening Therese had given some resistance to her mother, and her mother had insisted on obedience and the little girl was not therefore in very good humor when Mrs. Martin was putting her to bed. Of the sequel, Mrs. Martin writes to Pauline, December 5th, 1875: "After she had gone to bed, she called to me that she had not said her prayers. I replied, 'Go to sleep and you can say them tomorrow.' But she was not satisfied. To put an end to the trouble, her father went to her and heard her prayers. But she still was not satisfied; she wanted to say some other prayer that we couldn't understand. Finally, your father gathered something of what she meant, and said the prayer, and then we had peace until the next morning."

Vain and futile details, some one will say. Yes, if we were dealing with an ordinary infant. But what Christian will deny the interest of investigating the first traces of the divine influx on a soul which was to become such a furnace of supernatural love? And besides these letters picture the mother as well as Therese, and to picture the mother is the purpose of this book.

Therese is now nearly three years old and delights her mother by her progress in the little lessons she took with Celine. The mother writes to Pauline: "Therese has an intelligence such as I have never observed in any of you when you were so young."

Mrs. Martin now recalls her ambition as a young mother, "all her children consecrated to God"—what a joy! Marie, her first child, simple and modest and serious, now began to show indications of a vocation to the life of the cloister. Pauline had not become vain because of her constant scholarly successes, but was obedient and industrious and even more faithful to her exercises of piety than to her studies. This news from the Visitation school was a source of greatest joy to Mrs. Martin. She wrote to Pauline, December 5, 1875: "You are my true friend. You give me courage to endure life with patience. Be always the joy to others that you have been to me. The good God will bless you not only in the next world, but in this, because he is always happiest even in this life, who always bravely does his duty."

Mrs. Martin had, too, her own happy dreams. She gave over her rare hours of leisure to spiritual reading, reading that revealed the joys of religious life, joys which she had ambitioned as a girl and which attracted her still and to which she wished to lead her daughters. She wrote to Pauline, September 5, 1875: "I am reading the life of the holy Chantal. I am ravished with admiration. It is the more interesting to me because I love the Visitation. How happy are they who are called! I dream sometimes of the cloister and solitude. I do not know really, considering the ideas I have, why it was not my vocation to remain either an old maid or to enter a convent. I would now like to live to be very old so that when my children are all grown up, I could retire to the solitude of the convent."

Alas, these hopes of a long life and of an old age spent in the cloister were not to be attained. God had other designs on this wonderful woman who had already prepared for Him, from afar, five religious. By the merit of her sufferings heroically borne, she had formed the character of Marie and Pauline and by her intercession she was to obtain for the little Therese the graces which would make her one day a great saint, "the most pure victim of Merciful Love."

VI

The Mother's Influence Upon St. Therese

"All my life," writes the Little Flower, "it has pleased our Lord to surround me with affection. My earliest recollections are of loving smiles and of tender caresses; but if He made others love me so much, He made me love them too, for I was of an affectionate nature."

The influence of these holy affections and of those domestic virtues, of which the Little Flower has testified in the passage just quoted, Therese gives as the reason for her early attraction to all that is good and holy.

Let us note how some other acts which were performed by her parents daily before the eyes of Therese, acts which could not but develop in her, little by little, a high sense of duty.

The patience of the father, his charity to the servants and employees, his high sense of justice, all this we may be sure did not escape the little Therese, keen little observer as she always

69

was. Then, too, the parents always observed strictly the Sunday rest, and kept rigorously the fasts of the Church, and the mother went much farther than the Church requires in penance and mortification. For instance, when Mrs. Martin, eight months before her death, was to undergo an operation of which we will speak later, she refused to take supper on the eve of the operation, saying that it was an Ember day and she wished to keep the fast.

We might expect that to such a devout mother manifestations of the supernatural world would not be lacking and indeed when I was at Mrs. Martin's home, talking with the custodian, Mrs. Grant, the latter, in answer to my remark that it must be a great consolation to live always in the Little Flower's home, replied, "Oh yes, there were miracles in this house." And then she related this story: "You remember," she said, "with what tenderness Mrs. Martin loved the little Helene, who died at the age of five years. Well, one day shortly after Helene's death, Mrs. Martin remembered a little fib that Helene once told in the course of a childish conversation, and Mrs. Martin immediately went to the statue of the Blessed Virgin in her home and begged that if the little Helene were being kept in purgatory because of that little fib that the Blessed Mother would release her. Immediately, in answer to her prayer, a voice issued from the statue,* saying "Helene is here—here at my side."

Such then were the exemplary lives constantly before Therese as models. Therese observed them closely and admired them greatly and loved them ardently. She tells us in her autobiography: "You can hardly imagine how much I loved my father and mother, and, being very demonstrative, I showed my love in a thousand little ways, though the means I employed make me smile now when I think of them."

Aided and stimulated by this ardent affection, the piety of Therese increased day by day. She wished always to please her parents; she knew they were so perfect because they loved

*This statue had been given to Mr. Martin before his marriage by a pious person of Alencon who had a reputation for sanctity. It is the same statue that later smiled upon and cured the Little Flower. [Author's Note.]

God so much; and so she comprehended very early in life that one must love greatly the good God, do all that He commands, avoid all that He forbids and she brought to this work of loving God, all the ardor of her intense nature. When her reason first began to function, it occupied itself with eternal problems. The little child, for instance, was beginning to comprehend that eternal happiness is a recompense and that therefore one must earn it, merit it. Of this, Mrs. Martin writes: "Therese tells me this morning that she wishes to go to Heaven, and that therefore she would always be as good as a little angel."

Therese had such a high notion of God's goodness that she thought, in her ingenuity, that He, even when offended, would not separate a child from its mother; hence, this naive dialogue reported by Mrs. Martin, October 29, 1876, in a letter to Pauline: "Therese (then three years old) said to me, 'Mama, will I go to Heaven?' 'Yes, if you are good,' I told her. 'Oh Mama,' she answered, 'then if I am not good shall I go to Hell? Then, I know what I shall do: I shall fly to you in Heaven, and you will hold me tight in your arms and how could God take

me away then.' I saw that she was convinced that God could do nothing to her if she hid herself in my arms."

Another letter of Mrs. Martin's to Pauline showed how Therese served to alleviate her heavy burden: "My little Therese is my happiness. She will be good; I can see that already. She speaks only of God. She wouldn't for all the world miss her prayers. I wish you could hear her. Never have I seen anything so charming."

This family so intimately united, this atmosphere so amiable and sanely joyous and yet so holy and religious with faith animating all their relations and penetrating all their acts, could not but react strongly on the character of Therese. Therese expresses this negatively in her Autobiography when she says, "I am sure that had I been brought up by careless parents, I should have become very wicked and perhaps have lost my soul." Conversely, the facts are that she was brought up by superbly Christian parents and therefore became very holy and saved not only her own soul, but countless others. That is the theme and purpose of this book, the raison d'etre of every anecdote given herein, namely, to show that the holiness of the

Little Flower is due in no small degree to her parents, to the training they, and especially her saintly* mother, gave her. One day in Normandy I told the Little Flower's sister, Leonie, that I was going to write this book about her mother, and that the theme of the book would be that the mother was a saint and that her holiness, influence, training and prayers explained in no small degree the holiness of the Little Flower. Leonie declared that I was right in both propositions and gladly wrote that declaration so that it might be used in this book as a foreword.

Certainly after God it was to the living faith and example and devotion of her mother that Therese owed first her gentleness and then her detachment from pleasure, and finally her determination always to give pleasure, cost what it might, to the good Jesus, Whom she saw her dear mother loved so ardently.

We have passed in review some examples of piety, faith, devotion, courage and resigna-

*Wherever in this book the word "saint" is employed, it is used without any intention of anticipating the judgment of the Church. [Author's Note.]

75

tion in trial that the mother gave to the Little Therese. These examples would doubtless not have affected Therese so profoundly if the mother had not been as affectionate as she was solicitous. It was by love that, little by little, the mother formed Therese to love also, to love even to the giving of her whole self to God, to love even to great sacrifice and to death.

The tenderness of Mrs. Martin was not sentimental and soft but virile. She was a strong character, who for all the world would not attempt to flatter or pamper her children or to overlook in them a dangerous inclination; but at the same time, she knew how to bestow on them signs of the most tender and most moving affection. She herself relates with what affection and condescension she responded to the loving, childish desires of Therese. She writes Pauline: "Therese will not even go upstairs alone without calling me at each step, 'Mama, Mama,' and if I forget to answer 'Yes, darling,' she waits where she is and will not move."

Such was the education of love without softness that Therese received from her mother, and how much of the Little Flower's love of God and desire to please Him is due to that admirable training?

The photographs of the Little Flower's relatives were secured and given to Father Dolan by Leonie. They are reproduced in this book for the first time. [Author's Note.]

The Little Flower's Mother

VII

Twilight and Dawn

February 24, 1877, Mrs. Martin received this letter from the Visitation Convent at Mans: "This morning your well-beloved sister, Sister Mary Dosithee, ended her edifying life by a death worthy of envy. Her presence of mind, her serenity, her devotion were admirable to the end."

"Now," wrote Mrs. Martin to her brother, "we have one more protector in Heaven, for it would be difficult to close more holily so virtuous a life as our sister's."

This hope sustained Mrs. Martin in the sorrow the sad news caused her. She asked her children, especially Therese, to beg daily the heavenly protection of their aunt. Mrs. Martin herself prayed that the intercession of her pious sister, joined to that of the Blessed Virgin, would bring about a miracle of which she herself had need, as we shall now see.

When Mrs. Martin was a young girl, she
had an accident; she fell violently and struck her
breast against the corner of a table. The result
was a lump, at first not very painful, but ultimately the lump became a decaying fibrous
tumor, which, I suppose, we would call cancer.
Without ever complaining, without interrupting
her fatiguing labors, without omitting any religious or family duties, Mrs. Martin had borne
valiantly for more than sixteen years the pain of
this tumor, which was slowly doing its work of
destruction. When the pain so increased that
she could no longer hide her state from her dear
ones, they called a doctor of Alencon, Doctor
Prevost, who seeing the hopelessness of the case
gave her, for form's sake, a prescription. "What
is this for?" asked Mrs. Martin. And the doctor
said sadly, "It is to console the sick."

Mrs. Martin's brother advised an operation and for this purpose brought his sister to a
celebrated surgeon in Lisieux who declared, "It
is too late."

Condemned by the doctors, and having
the prospect of dying in the midst of the greatest
suffering, the courageous Christian returned to
Alencon, took up again her ordinary life and

had no other thought than to perform, to the end, without weakness or ostentation, her daily duties.

She wrote to her brother's wife, January 28, 1877: "You are too much concerned about me, my dear sister. I am not worried. I do not deserve that you should be so concerned about me; my life is not so precious."

Soon she gave up her lace business, and wrote, "I love the work and regret to give it up, but I can easily live on our income."

The image of death had become familiar to her; she could face it without trembling, but she thought that, since her Visitation Sister was dead, her daughters needed her to superintend their education, so she begged her sister in Heaven and the Blessed Virgin to give her back her health, and to this end she made in June, 1877, a pilgrimage to Lourdes. Marie, Pauline and Leonie accompanied her because she hoped that the urgent prayers of her pious children joined to her own would obtain from Mary Immaculate her cure.

The journey was more fatiguing than had been foreseen. Insufficient warmth, poor food and the difficulty of finding suitable lodging in Lourdes all contributed to make her condition worse. She plunged four times into the water of the sacred pool of Lourdes, but alas her pains were not alleviated. Once home she wrote to her brother's wife, June 24, 1877: "I would have been doubly happy to have been cured, because of the happiness it would have caused you, but alas the Blessed Mother has said to us as she did to Bernadette: 'I will make you happy, not in this world, but in the next.'"

On the return journey from Lourdes to Alencon, Mrs. Martin joined the other pilgrims in chanting with full voice the customary hymns—this in the presence of her daughters, silent, sad and despondent.

Her husband, with Celine and Therese, met the train. They had passed a difficult week, always expecting a happy message that never

*Many of the facts concerning Mrs. Martin, reported in these pages, were told to me by Leonie, the Little Flower's sister; others were found in a French book recommended to me by Pauline. The book is entitled "La Vie de Saint Therese," by Laveille, to whom I am greatly indebted. [Author's Note.]

arrived. The husband was, of course, saddened, and Celine and Therese were astounded that the Blessed Virgin had not heeded their innocent prayers. Mr. Martin was surprised to see his wife return as gaily as if she had obtained the grace that she desired.

"That attitude of mine," wrote Mrs. Martin to her sister-in-law, "gave him new courage, and my resignation brought good cheer to the household."

The cheerful attitude of Mrs. Martin was assumed out of pure charity towards her loved ones. To her daughter Pauline, whose piety the mother knew and whom she wished to habituate to facing trouble, Mrs. Martin wrote her true sentiments. Her letter to Pauline read: "Are you still angry with our Blessed Mother because she did not make you dance with joy?... Do not look for much joy on earth, for if you do you will be disappointed. As for me, I know by experience to what extent to rely on the joys of earth and if I did not live only for the joys of Heaven, I would indeed now be miserable."

Nevertheless, to console her dear ones, and to maintain her own courage, the poor mother continued to pray for a miracle. She wished once more to visit at Lisieux her brother's family, which had always been so dear and helpful to her. She planned on bringing Celine and Therese with her, and writing to her sister-in-law about their keen desire of accompanying her, Mrs. Martin said in her letter of July 8, 1877: "The youngest (Therese) will be the most impressed by the journey. She will remember all her life that when she was two years old, we left her home when we went to visit you, and when she speaks of it now, the tears always come. She is a charming little creature, my little Therese. I assure you that she will amount to something."

The little child who wished to be taken along on a visit to Lisieux could not of course foresee the cruel event that would prevent the journey.

Relentlessly, the disease progressed. The months of July and August were marked by intolerable pain; no sleep, no peace, no rest for the invalid on her bed of suffering where she passed most of her twenty- four hours.

She saw clearly the gravity of her own condition and with that faith which had been the light and consolation of her life, she prepared herself for the inevitable. She wrote on

July 15, 1877 to her sister-in-law: "I have resigned myself to my fate. It is absolutely necessary that I lose nothing of the little time that
remains for me to live. These are the days of
salvation that will never return; I wish to profit
by them."

To assure herself of the grace of final
perseverance, and to give to the end to her
family an example of fidelity to religious duties,
she dragged herself for the last time, the first
Friday in August, to the morning mass in the
parish church. At each step, her breast and neck
were pierced as with a dagger. Acute pains in
the entire right side obliged her frequently to
stop and rest. Nevertheless she went on and in
this condition heard the entire mass and drew
from the Sacrifice of Calvary renewed on the
Altar courage to meet the last struggle.

The following weeks saw the progres-
sive dissolution of the poor body which col-
lapsed under the action of the implacable disease. Thoughtful of her daughters to the end,
she determined to spare Celine and Therese the
sight of her pain and arranged to send them
during the day to the home of friends. Therese,
in the following passage from her Autobiogra-

phy, gives us her memories of these days:

"All the details of my mother's illness are still fresh in my mind. I remember especially her last weeks on earth when Celine and I felt like little exiles. Every morning a friend came to fetch us and we spent the day with her. Once we had not the time to say our prayers before starting, and on the way my little sister whispered, 'Must we tell her that we have not said our prayers?' 'Yes,' I answered. So very timidly Celine confided our secret to her and she exclaimed, 'Well, children, you shall say them.' Then she took us to a large room and left us there. Celine looked at me in amazement. I was equally astonished and exclaimed, 'This is not like Mama, she always said our prayers with us.' During the day, in spite of all efforts to amuse us, the thought of our dear mother was constantly in our minds, and I remember that my sister once had an apricot given to her and she leaned towards me and said, 'We will not eat it, I will give it to Mama.' Alas, our beloved mother was much too ill to eat any earthly fruit; she would never more be satisfied but by the glory of Heaven. There she would drink the mysterious Wine with Jesus at His Last Supper,

to share with us in the Kingdom of His Father."

One more day of earthly joy was reserved for the mother. Marie, who had been the tutor of Celine and Therese that year, decided that since vacation had come that they would have closing exercises at home, just as in the public and private schools. To encourage her sisters and to distract the mother, a distribution of prizes was arranged. Marie writes to her aunt, "I assure you that it was all very beautiful. The room was ornamented with garlands of roses. The presidents of the august ceremony were Mr. and Mrs. Martin. Yes, my dear aunt, Mama also wished to assist. Celine and Therese were dressed in white and would that you could have seen with what triumphant manner they received the prizes which Papa and Mama distributed."

It was the last smile the family gave to her who was about to leave them. Eight days later she wrote to her brother, August 16: "My strength is gone. If the Blessed Virgin does not cure me, it is because my time is come, and the good God wishes me to rest with Him in Heaven."

On the 26th of the same month, Mrs.

Martin was given Holy Viaticum, and Mr. Martin himself, walking before the priest with the Blessed Sacrament, bore the candle from the church to the home into which our Lord entered to fortify his dying servant for the last journey. Therese was present and guessed the coming solemn separation, but believed that her heroic mother, even though she was returning to God, would not entirely abandon her dear little daughter.

Therese writes in her Autobiography: "The touching ceremony of Extreme Unction made a deep impression on me. I can still see the place where I knelt, and hear my poor father's sobs."

Mrs. Martin, so well prepared, broke the ties that bound her to earth on August 28th, 1877, at midnight. She was 46 years old. Twilight had given place to the Dawn! Who can doubt that she went straight to Heaven?

Therese writes: "The day after her death, my father took me in his arms, and said, 'Come and kiss your dear mother for the last time.' Without saying a word, I put my lips to her icy forehead. I do not remember having cried much, but I did not talk to anyone of all that filled my heart. I looked and listened in silence and I saw many things which they would have hidden from me. Once I found myself close to the coffin in the passage. I stood looking at it for a long time. I had never seen one before, but I knew what it was. I was so small that I had to lift my head to see its full length and it seemed to be very big, and very sad."

After the funeral, the family returned to their home and Therese writes: "We were all five together, looking at one another sadly, when our nurse, overcome with emotion, said, turning to Celine and to me, 'Poor little dears; you no longer have a mother.' Then Celine threw herself into Marie's arms crying, 'Well, you will be my mother now.' I was so accustomed to imitating Celine that I should have undoubtedly followed her example, but I feared Pauline would be sad, and feel herself left out that she too had not a little daughter, so, with a loving look, I hid my face on her breast, saying in my turn, 'And Pauline will be my mother.'"*

*Zelie had, as she was dying, indicated her wish that Pauline assume the maternal mission, from which God was taking her. [Author's Note.]

The days following the funeral were indeed lonely and sad. The family left the house only once and then to go to the cemetery. Mr. Martin sold his business and property and determined to move to Lisieux, where Mrs. Martin's brother and sister-in-law to whom Mrs. Martin had been so attached, might give him and Pauline the benefit of their advice, counsel and help in bringing up the little motherless children. On the following 5th of September, the Martin family moved into the famous Buissonetts at Lisieux, where Therese was to find her vocation to the Carmel of Lisieux and there reach the summit of heroic sanctity.

Mrs. Martin's body was later brought to the Lisieux cemetery and she and her husband were buried together there. When I knelt before her tomb, I could not bring myself to pray for her, but rather to her.

So, dear reader, do you say a prayer to this holy woman whose life mirrored in these pages has, I hope, taught you lessons which it would be superfluous for me to formulate. We may be sure that not only Therese, but her mother are in Heaven now and that they are ready and anxious to help all those who wish to imitate them. That they will help all my readers to follow in their footsteps is the author's constant prayer.

finis

Publisher's Note:

For more information about the cause of Louis and Zelie
Martin please write The Martin Guild c/o The Firefly Press.

Also from The Firefly Press:

THE CHEERFUL CHERUB MAGAZINE
 A little magazine devoted to the Catholic family
AND THESE THY GIFTS
A Cheerful Cherub Readers Cookbook
THE YEAR AND OUR CHILDREN
 Mary Reed Newland
ROMAN CATHOLIC RESOURCE GUIDE
Kaye Harker-Hansen

Forthcoming Titles in 1995

MY NAMEDAY - COME FOR DESSERT
Helen McLoughlin
COOKING FOR CHRIST
Florence Berger

The Firefly Press
P.O. Box 262302
San Diego, CA 92196